DITCHING PRINCIPLES

By

"Bry the Dunker Guy"
Bryan Webster

Note for Librarians: A cataloguing record for this book is available from Library and Archives Canada at www.collectionscanada.ca/amicus/index-e.html
ISBN 1-4120-6902-5

Printed in Victoria, BC, Canada. Printed on paper with minimum 30% recycled fibre. Trafford's print shop runs on "green energy" from solar, wind and other environmentally-friendly power sources.

Offices in Canada, USA, Ireland and UK
This book was published *on-demand* in cooperation with Trafford Publishing. On-demand publishing is a unique process and service of making a book available for retail sale to the public taking advantage of on-demand manufacturing and Internet marketing. On-demand publishing includes promotions, retail sales, manufacturing, order fulfilment, accounting and collecting royalties on behalf of the author.

Book sales for North America and international:
Trafford Publishing, 6E–2333 Government St.,
Victoria, BC v8t 4p4 CANADA
phone 250 383 6864 (toll-free 1 888 232 4444)
fax 250 383 6804; email to orders@trafford.com
Book sales in Europe:
Trafford Publishing (uk) Limited, 9 Park End Street, 2nd Floor
Oxford, UK oxi 1hh UNITED KINGDOM
phone 44 (0)1865 722 113 (local rate 0845 230 9601)
facsimile 44 (0)1865 722 868; info.uk@trafford.com
Order online at:
trafford.com/05-1813

10 9 8 7 6

The content of this book is meant to assist pilots and passengers on how to Egress from aircraft involved in a ditching.

Information for this was collected from a variety of sources and is believed to be beneficial when used in the way suggested.

All people involved in aircraft accidents or incidents respond differently to real life challenges or threatening situations.

Bryan Webster, Aviation Egress Systems and its employees can not be held responsible for any situations associated with materials used from the contents or procedures of this guide.

TABLE OF CONTENTS

ACKNOWLEDGMENTS

I would like to thank all involved in the support and encouragement for the completion of this book on a previously not well documented subject.

As a long term fixed wing aircraft pilot I saw a need to help aid future aviators recognize the hazards of a ditching, and how to act in a positive manner should this happen to them personally.

A special thanks to my wife Patti plus many fellow aviators and friends who helped supply not only information but also moral support.

CHAPTER ONE

Bry the Dunker Guy

As a child born in the late 1950's at Burkeville a small community which is located under the flight path of the Canadian owned Vancouver BC International airport, I had little airplanes flowing through my veins at an early age.Prior to my starting grade one our family of 5 moved to nearby Richmond which offered me a new vantage point for viewing aircraft from a mile south instead of upwards at the wheel wells.

Years rolled by with my building the typical balsa wood models like most young boys, then motorized with strings to test how long you could fly circles standing in one spot before falling over.

Once realizing radio controllers were the way to go in the early 70's I learned how a person could spend all available cash supplies on kits and gear required for free flight, only to watch the crash and disintegration shortly after takeoff. Over many more years of trial and error I created a huge supply depot of odds and sods for toy aircraft parts and eventually managed to master countless R/C flights on wheels, skis and floats.

Then one day in the spring of 1975 a friend of the family offered me a ride in his 1966 Cessna 150 hangared at the Pitt Meadows airport only an hour's drive east. Soon after I found myself on the roll from runway 25 and heading up over the North Shore Mountains flying towards the community of Squamish BC where later in life I would find work in a sawmill to finance my pilots license.

After an hour or so in the air I was put to the test while upside down in loops spins and rolls until my stomach could no longer take it, and I was handed a barf bag so as not to spill my guts all over the inside of his precious aircraft. Back on ground in spite of the ill feeling, plus weak knees I was hooked on the new found freedom of flight and looking forward to going again.

For many weekends to follow I would anxiously wait for the opportunity of yet another flight, and my enthusiasm must have been contagious as we became regulars at the airport coffee shop after a day of flying. In short order I learned how to wash bugs off the wings and vacuum inside the 150 airframe, which eventually led to helping maintain the little bird and before long I was merrily in the right seat learning the basics of flight. With boundless energy and curiosity investigating every aircraft on the field I learned what went on around small airfields and soon became one of the regular airport groupies.

With all that time being spent around the local flyers it was not long before being asked when I was going to get serious about flying, meaning take off the training wheels and sign up for lessons at the local flight school.

My biggest obstacle, beside the lack of required funds at that time was the fact that my birthday was in the fall and Transport Canada had an age requirement I just could not find a way around.

Patiently I waited for my 16th birthday to be eligible for lessons on a mid 1940 Fleet Canuck tail dragger that was one of three operated by the school, where they still believed pilots were better trained in this configuration.

Over the summer and into fall my right seat time was building and I had experienced many local flights and trips to nearby airports plus islands giving me an advantage for when real training started.

Finally my day arrived and soon after the walk around to learn about fabric and cotter pin locations I was puttering out towards the run up ramp. After the usual checks and assurances all is well we taxied to the active and commenced take off thus starting the required circuits stalls steep turns and emergencies for 13 hours until solo day. Then on that afternoon I recall looking at the lonely right seat which I had recently moved out of as I roared down the runway and leapt into the air in what felt like a jet fighter due to the loss of instructor's weight. Over the following months I drove out to the airport for weekly missions honing my skills over farmer fields and Pitt Lake, marveling at the realization that I was alone and soaring around building time and experience.

About then I was ready for a cross country and more advanced flight training when another locally owned 1966 Cessna 150 went up for sale, so I decided to buy half with a partner thus saving the remaining hours for my own aircraft. Now a proud half owner in a two-seat toy I hired an instructor to finish my private license that allowed me to roam further in my flights without the structure of a school environment and with more freedom to explore. At this point I was on my students permit and had no great desire to finish my license as I was already flying all over the place and having a ball until wanting to share my new found love with passengers.

For that winter and into spring my training had been sadly neglected but with summer around the corner and anxious to haul people I got back into the ground school studies and preparing for the almighty exam and flight test. I buckled down and did as all good flight students do and started reading our famous pilots book "From the Ground up" on regulations, navigation and weather sections for what seemed like eternity.

Then on the afternoon of August 26 1977 my old family friend offered me a break from studies, so away we went to practice aerobatics and joy ride in his machine which had just been freshly washed and needed drying off.

Soon we were airborne and over the town of Mission a few miles east of our location upside down and twirling about in loops snap rolls and his favorite configuration the spin.

Being much more accustomed to flying in general I enjoyed the maneuvers and was able to keep my emotions under control through out the entire event, until we were finished and heading west for home base.

Our routing followed the mighty Fraser River directly, and as it was a calm clear evening the pilot elected to get down low and enjoy the sights close up waving to the fisherman standing on the shores and watching farmers in their fields. Then as we came low around a bend in the river and flew between the shore and an island straight into the setting sun we were confronted with 16 unmarked power lines draped across our path, ranging from 20 to 100 feet above water. I remember looking left at the Captain, who had also just noted our predicament as he was attempting to instinctively pull up and go over top of them, but he realized it was too late and that plan would have been hopeless. I looked ahead again only to see that we were almost in the black strands so away we go straight down, nearly clipping each wire with our antennas until we ducked under the bottom one leading us to safety. Unfortunately as it turned out we needed another 10 feet elevation which was not available, and due to the sharp rotation required to duck under the bottom wire we hit the water surface flat at well over 100 MPH thus beginning my advanced training in aviation - Egress.

Unmarked wire span from left shore to island over the Fraser River.

Cessna 150 wreckage is the white dot behind boat.
Wires and towers still barely visible

Cessna 150 aircraft wreckage being towed to Pitt Meadows floatplane
ramp Aug. 1977

Remains of the Cessna 150

CHAPTER TWO

Egress

Egress - Emergence, place or means of going out exit or opening, passage; escape route or way out.

Planning for an aircraft Egress starts at the airport or floatplane dock before you ever enter any aircraft type or configuration that you as pilot may find yourself in command. What I will try to explain here is not to fear aircraft or what could happen during any given flight, but to respect and understand the perils of an unexpected ditching.

Each year in Canada and around the world pilots, for a wide variety of reasons end up ditching in the water that we so often fly over with out any pre-determined escape plan. It could be a floatplane striking an object while on takeoff and capsizing, possibly a wheel equipped aircraft lifting off a runway out over water with unexpected mechanical difficulties, or either one over huge swells and out of fuel.

The actual reason an aircraft with pilot and possibly passengers onboard finds themselves ditching is irrelevant, what is done prior to and in the first few seconds after the crash is what dictates disaster or a positive outcome.

In this book I refuse to spout off a bunch of statistics as to how many people survive or perish a ditching because depending on the aircraft configuration, water temperature and the agency responsible for the information there are vast differences.

For example here in Canada our water temperatures fluctuate dramatically from one season to another.

In mid summer there will be beaches covered with sun worshippers and swimmers enjoying the warm comfortable water conditions all day.

Then only a few months later you will witness the same people strolling along at that identical location wrapped up in heavy clothing, gloves scarves and toques with red wind burned faces.

The difference in temperature is similar to an aircraft ditching in the warm waters of the Caribbean mid January, and then on the same day another aircraft succumbing to a water impact in the Pacific Ocean.

For the Pacific Ocean people the fact our body temperatures are roughly 98.6 degrees Fahrenheit and then being rapidly submerged into liquid 50 degrees colder, the shock is overwhelming and may even take their breath away. For the folks experiencing a similar ditching into the Caribbean waters their bodies are also 98.6 degrees Fahrenheit, and yet they take little notice of the minor ocean temperature gradient and focus on the Egress as their water experience may be closer in comparison to a warm bath.

Simply put the colder the water temperature the higher the risk of fatalities due to our body's initial response when subjected to large changes of temperature. This sudden shock to the body distracts an individual from the real emergency of being trapped upside down in a sinking aircraft, thus wasting precious time in making good their escape.

To fully understand the panic and disorientation associated with this subject you could only have been involved in some similar underwater emergency; books and theories are great teachers, but true Egress training must involve a swimming pool and specialized equipment.

Next time you are planning a flight, head out a few minutes earlier and spend just a little time to become more familiar with exits and emergency equipment which you may have to depend on one day.

The first thing to consider is are all your cargo and baggage doors unlocked prior to flight allowing access to the aircraft interior from the outside. These could be used to gain access by good samaritans or rescue personnel in the event of a crash as most aircraft doors lock on the outside when you secure the door from the inside.

Take notice of all your window shapes and sizes including properties, meaning type of material they are constructed from be it Plexiglas, lexan or glass. In the case of light Plexiglas you may be able to smash out a side window with a solid kick, but lexan may prove to be more challenging. The front windows of a De Havilland Beaver for example are solid glass which could require a heavy blunt object to remove in an emergency. Other manufacturers have built their front windows out of Plexiglas which could possibly prove easier to smash, although the V bar tubes running at angles across your exit will restrict your egress or could make it impossible.

Test your Emergency Locator Transmitter occasionally as per the Canadian Aeronautical Information Publication (SAR) page 3-3 paragraph 3.8 on frequency 121.5 MHz. QUOTE: Any testing of an ELT must be conducted only during the first 5 minutes of any UTC hour and restricted in duration to not more than 5 seconds. Now before you finish ensure the G switch is in the arm position and ready to activate a distress signal upon an impact or sudden stop which immediately contacts specific search and rescue centers.

Depending on where you travel your survival kit could be lacking many essentials. It should contain the mandatory supplies for all on board consisting of food, matches and a mirror which could draw attention to your aircraft location and aid in an expedient rescue. For our Northern Canadian and Alaskan flyers however you may end up hundreds of miles from any community or civilization, and possibly days before anyone finds you due to poor weather. These more adventurous aviators should consider packing things relevant to wilderness survival such as an axe and sleeping bags, foil space blankets plus mosquito repellant or any other bush related amenities to make backwoods camping more enjoyable.

Today, with all of our new technologies and advancements my recommendation for a large number of our pilots is to consider a satellite phone which makes communications anywhere in the world possible when cell phones are out of range. Now inside your aircraft take a look around from a different point of view and the normal "belt up then go" routine; is the equipment you carry out of date or could you actually depend on what's there with your life in an emergency. The number one item of importance after any ditching is your life vest so the type and certification date is extremely important, especially if the aircraft sunk shortly after you departed and are faced with cold water and a swim to shore. Typically floatplanes carry the standard inflatable Transport Canada/FAA certified C-13 vest, which has most likely been stuffed in all the seat backs since the aircraft was originally purchased. News Flash, if they are older they will most likely fail to inflate when you need them most, or will leak air when inflated due to the sharp objects they have shared quarter with for the past 15 years. Now being a privately registered aircraft there is no requirement to have them inspected annually as do our commercial operators, but you may want to consider it at least every few years.

To ensure you know what is in the plastic pouch take one out and try one on, or better yet before sending them away for inspection consider replacing the works with a manual inflating Mustang model which is readily available and is worn comfortably during all flights.

By wearing the vest there is no chance of leaving it behind after you depart a sinking aircraft, which is one of the most common mistakes I personally have witnessed in my years as a water Egress instructor.

Next doors and handles should be studied for shapes and locations, as once scrambling about confused and disoriented plus out of breath is not the time to realize they are foreign objects to you.

There are a few aircraft out there with double rear exit doors which when flaps are extended for take off block the same door your passengers came in through moments earlier.

Think of this scenario for a moment; there are six seats onboard your wheeled aircraft designed in sections of two each and three rows front to back.

Your passengers in the front three seats get in via the front left door, as there is no door on the front right side and then buckle up awaiting departure. You now assist the back two passengers via the right rear doors and help them belt in prior to securing the doors and return to enter up front on the left side.

As you taxi out for departure and complete the checklist, flaps are lowered to 18 degrees and unknown to those two rear passengers they have just lost the ability for exiting the rear of the aircraft with ease once the flaps are extended and now block the doors path to swing open freely.

Shortly after departure from RWY 26 L you are out over the Pacific ocean and suddenly there is an engine failure at 500 feet, thus little time for communication to those on board and second's later "splash" you're soaked through upside down in cold water.

Instinctively as the pilot you release your seat belts and open the front door to Egress for the surface and breathe from the much needed fresh air, hopefully followed by the other 5 passengers in the aircraft who were beside and behind you. The problem here is the 2 folks in the back row came in via the right rear side doors, sat beside them and have full intentions of departing via those same doors, which are completely blocked by the extended flaps previously set for take off.

(Details in Appendix 1 on next page)

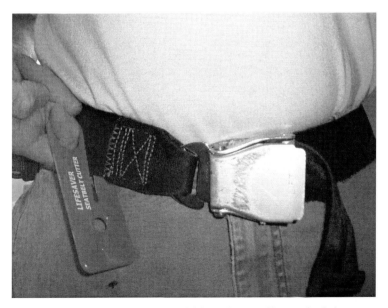

Seatbelt cutters are readily available and very effective for helping extricate persons trapped in aircraft with out worry of injury.

Appendix 1

In ASL 7/90, as a result of a safety information letter from the Canadian Aviation Safety Board, we showed the correct procedure for opening the doors with the flaps down. The procedure is repeated below, along with the original graphic, which clearly illustrates the difficulty:

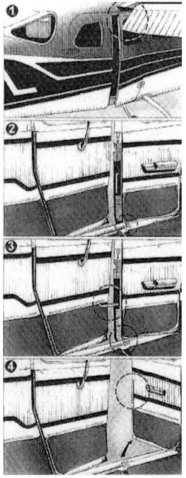

(a) unlatch the forward cargo door;

(b) open the forward cargo door as much as possible (about 3 in.) (figures 1 and 2);

(c) unlatch the rear cargo door by pulling down on the red handle (figure 2);

(d) partially open the rear door until the door latch at the base of the door is clear of the floor (figure 3);

(e) close the rear cargo door latch by placing the red handle into the well in the door jamb (the locking pins will now be extended, but clear of the fuselage); and

(f) push open the rear cargo door (figure 4).

Now this procedure is quite demanding for most people under normal circumstances. Picture this process in the dark with an inverted airplane, and rushing water with two or three distressed passengers trying to escape.

The Cessna 206 emergency-exit issue has been addressed extensively in the past by, among others, the TSB in 1985 and 1989; the ASL 7/90 article referred to above; Cessna service bulletin (SB) SEB91-04, issued on March 22, 1991; and many letters exchanged among the industry, Transport Canada (TC), the TSB and the Federal Aviation Administration (FAA) since the last two fatal accidents. In addition, you — the owners, operators and associations — are well aware of the problem.

The facts in this case are unfortunately this, human nature being what it is those two rear passengers will most likely perish due to drowning while trying desperately to open the cargo doors without thinking about moving forward and following everyone else to safety.

In the event you decide to dive back down and aid the two rear occupants bear in mind they are out of air and well into survival mode, thus you will be in great danger as they are panicked and extremely powerful.

The other concern for this same scenario is common in this type of aircraft. During the ditching portion of the emergency this aircraft often comes to a violent sudden stop hitting the water and inverting knocking the pilots head with sufficient force rendering him/her unconscious.

Now all 5 passengers are trapped and must find the elusive front left door handle located in the pilot's armrest which is upside down and hidden, only to be found with great luck or previous knowledge as to where it would be. Regarding the seat belts installed in your aircraft be it factory or an after market addition, are they adequate and in good working condition in the event they are ever seriously put to the test?

The older machines came equipped with a lap belt only, and believe me I tested that theory flying in the Yukon Territories in October 1985 during a total engine failure after take off one morning in a Cessna 180 on wheels. They were personally proven to me inadequate, because on entry into the tall poplar trees I found that the so called joystick gives you a false sense of security. With white knuckles you feel secure holding that sliding shaft until impact takes place, then you are thrust forward tied at the waist and your face becomes one with the knob littered dash board.

Had shoulder harnesses been available to me in that crash I would have had no injuries at all. Their not being installed put me in serious medical condition 80 miles from nowhere with a concussion and facial injuries.

Now you are most likely wondering if this guy is accident prone or crazy to continue in the profession that has threatened to kill him not once but twice. Think of it this way I was a commercial operator who lived and breathed aircraft seven days a week and was undaunted by the second occurrence, as it was really my first at the controls during an emergency after many thousands of successful flying hours.

In my first crash as a passenger the impact speed for the Cessna 150 was well over 100 MPH to dead stopped in the length of our little aircraft and I suffered only minor injuries due in part to the aerobatic style 5 point harnesses installed. The shoulder harnesses no doubt saved both our lives as the forces generated during that impact registered on the G meter and revealed we hit the stops both positive and negative.

Mechanical Accelerometers ("G" Meter) Register G forces acting on the airframe and occupants on board during aerobatic maneuvers or sudden stops. Each "G" indicates applied force.

Example – two "G" doubles body weight

That would explain why our chest areas under the belts were substantially bruised. On an impact of that magnitude with out shoulder harnesses we would have sustained major head injuries, or been knocked unconscious and drowned as the aircraft sunk shortly after we exited. In my second crash with the Cessna 180

I was at a considerably lower airspeed during impact, roughly 60 MPH, yet my injuries took months to overcome and I almost lost my right eye due to the lack of restraint that the shoulder harnesses are designed to provide.

As for the typical single strap you pull across your chest and snap to the waist belt attachment, they are better that nothing at all but I personally endorse the two straps over your shoulders and secured behind your head. Now with over 25 years experience and in excess of 10.000 hours flying time to date, when comparing my two personal incidents both the Cessna 150 crash with water, and Cessna 180 crash in the bush, I came to the conclusion that I seriously dislike unnecessary pain and thus will avoid it all costs.

So here we are all set to go flying for the day to our favorite lake or airstrip in our prized possession with 3 of our buddies one of which has never flown before. It would be prudent to have everyone briefed on doors and where the first aid kit is stored but there is one thing in particular which often is overlooked.

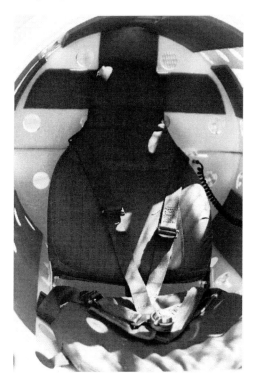

Cessna 180 Crashed at Ballarat Creek Yukon Oct 04/85

Post investigation revealed a blocked carburetor air intake
causing a total engine failure resulting in a deadstick
landing short of runway.

Be sure everyone has their seat belts on snugly around their hips, and in particular be certain the release latch is facing out and not rolled over which would be extremely difficult to undo in an emergency.

Today, most automobiles have seatbelts which snap together and release on your right hip, non-flyers do not have the same understanding of what we pilots take for granted. With our AES ditch training program my experience is a high percentage of passengers have great difficulty releasing their seat belts once upside down in our equipment. The reason is simple; non-flyers even when reminded immediately prior to the roll over in our pool course equipment instinctively reach for their hip to release the seat belt. Once unsuccessful in locating the buckle, they panic and use both hands still failing to find the release located in their mid section while precious time is being wasted.

Now taxiing out on the water check your controls 6 ways confirming complete and total unobstructed movement and the control locks internal and external have been removed, also that there is nothing on the right front seat hindering the pull back motion for the take off portion of flight. On floats, once lined up for departure and ready to add power take a good look ahead for debris or obstructions plus any possible wind gusts. In the event you are departing from a short lake or airstrip have a plan for the abort and when your PNR (point of no return) will be initiated if required, this way there are no surprises such as when the trees are coming at you and your heart rate goes ballistic. OK, now you are roaring down the runway or across the water with that feeling of anticipation prior to flight and things are looking good, moments later you're airborne with a big smile and you are on the way home or to the cabin. Remember one thing, your flight has just begun and statistics show take off and landing phases of flight are where the majority of accidents occur, so remain vigilant and constantly stay on top of the situation with emergency backups in mind until in level flight.

An example of things going bad and becoming one with the statistics would be in the unlikely event you hit a submerged log just under the water surface known as a deadhead on the water run, or had an engine failure shortly after lift off from the runway out over a lake. Here you are with passenger's onboard and very little time to communicate right before what will prove to be very traumatic and possibly life threatening situation for everyone involved. Little of what was discussed in your briefing will be remembered after the initial impact, but hopefully they will be able to locate the door handles upside down and under water allowing all to Egress safely.

This is where the real panic and high anxiety will be in full force, with bodies darting about frantically searching for an exit and hopefully succeeding, which would then allow for that mad dash to the water surface for the mandatory breath of air.

Once an aircraft has succumbed to a sudden stop and water inversion all on board individually go directly into survival mode. Without Egress training this proves to be chaotic and disorganized and often ends up with fatalities. First the ones managing to release their seat belts while upside down roll upright and become totally disoriented and then overwhelmed searching in vain for something recognizable.

To watch from the outside you would bear witness to hands darting about searching aimlessly for door handles or anything that would allow release from this underwater cage they so desperately wish to vacate.

At this same time when there are multiples of people involved, shoes and boots are thrashing about injuring each other as heart rates skyrocket intensifying the immediate demand for air to replenish their lungs.

Egress training in this situation would have prepared them mentally for an accident in a warm pool with lifeguards present and specialized equipment allowing for a progression to this stage with a solid understanding of how to react effectively.

They would have known to stay in their seatbelts upside down while attempting to open the door or window exit first, and then hold onto the open door frame securely before releasing the seatbelt preventing disorientation.

Regarding door handles, most people are unaware that when an aircraft has inverted the seat and door handles are in the proper orientation until such a time that the individual leaves their position.

Once the person releases the safety belt they automatically rotate underwater reversing the handles mechanics, where lifting opened the door previously now the opposite applies.

With all that adrenaline pumping through their veins and then feeling of entrapment underwater, there is no problem for the individual to simply tear the door handle off going in the wrong direction and limiting any chance for survival.

Many of the older aircraft have these handles on the inside door panels which simply lift to open, and return to center when closed or locked. The problem being that it is very easy to strip the center casting material rendering the handle useless once rotated the wrong way.

To better understand what I am referring to, sit in an aircraft with this style of handle and imagine pushing down on it with superhuman force, I am sure you will see my point.

Year's later manufacturers started putting them in armguards saving this from happening, which was wise although now they can be nearly impossible to find in the same inverted underwater state.

For ditch training candidates with multiple past dunks to their credit, they will be more comfortable overall and should even instinctively grab onto an inflatable life vest before departing the sinking ship, thus having the ability to swim longer distances such as to shore which could be invaluable.

Today's departure however was uneventful and we climbed up to altitude, leveled off and enjoyed the scenery from our birds eye view at 5000 feet en route our destination a few hours further north.

Earlier I stated the majority of accidents take place during landings and on take off where there is little time to react and deal with aircraft emergencies. Today though let's say we are extremely unlucky and run into an on route situation.

Our Cessna 172 on wheels with pilot and 3 is now 75 miles from landing at destination and descending through 2500 feet at night half way across a fairly large lake. The weather is good VFR with a solid ceiling above making the fall evening seem darker than usual with limited vision of ground contours.

The route flown has taken us far from all airport amenities

and we have not seen any form of life including towns, or light from automobiles traveling the roads in quite some time.

Suddenly the engine RPM begins to drop from 2400 to 1200 and then surges erratically with no explanation. Sustaining altitude becomes a problem and with large hills ahead it is evident we are not going to clear them or make our strip just 38 minutes further ahead as planned.

Right away your basic pilot emergency training is put to good use checking mag switches and fuel selectors for proper position, then scanning the gauges for fuel contents and oil pressures only to find everything except the engine power surges are normal.

Going from the frying pan and into the fire seconds later without warning and in spite of your best efforts to solve this problem, the engine slows rapidly and then quits completely.

It takes a moment for you realize this situation is for real and a feeling of vulnerability comes over you just before one of your passengers asks what's going on.

At this point there are a number of check list items and things in general you should do in the short time available which will ultimately make or break the event for you and your passengers.

In a perfect world reading directions and complying with them will give positive results, but in aviation there are so many variables, possibly in hundreds of different aircraft types nothing is 100 % guaranteed.

Given the gravity (no pun intended) of the situation only the person at the controls may truly understand how serious the minutes or seconds which lie ahead may be to all involved, and why certain decisions are made or not at that time under extreme stress.

Once it is evident that there is no chance of re-start and all possibilities have been exhausted you must face sobering facts, the shore possibly miles ahead is unattainable and a ditching is now the only possibility.

Listed below is a generic set of responses on what tasks must be performed in this type of situation. Your aircraft could be more complex thus may have demands such as retractable gear or door configurations to consider, so use this information as a guideline not gospel.

PREPARE FOR DITCHING

-FLY THE AIRCRAFT:
Once airspeed bleeds off below 100 MPH lower the nose and fly the airspeed suggested in your POH giving the best rate of descent.

-TRANSMIT:
MAYDAY MAYDAY MAYDAY on any frequency which could bring a response from other aviators or flight service station. As time could be very limited try anything including frequency 121.5MHz or even have passengers attempt calling out on cell and Sat phones with location and details.

-ELT:
Set to ON if dash mounted switch is available.

-TRANSPONDER:
Set to 7700

-SELECT THE DITCH LOCATION:
Preferably straight ahead, but in the event land or a boat is available within gliding range, head that direction.

-BRIEF THE CREW/ PASSENGERS:
Locate and donn the life vests without inflating, and detail the brace position. Remove ties plus any jewelry which could restrain movements while egressing.

-OPEN EXIT DOORS:
Open cabin doors and then put handle down keeping doors outside the airframe and unable to jam in door frames during impact. If this fails due to style of door mechanism jam an object such a VFR flight supplement in the bottom of the door to hold it open slightly.

-SECURE LOOSE ARTICLES:
Remove headset and glasses prior to impact, and stow all objects
which may impede or complicate your EGRESS.

-RESTRAINT SYSTEM:
Lock your shoulder harness recoil if installed and tighten lap belts
on everyone ensuring the buckle is facing outward and there are
no twists in any of the belts.

Front seat passengers with shoulder harness should cross their
arms at chest height and hold both straps tightly with hands not
letting fingers get between straps and their body.

Rear seat passengers should hold the seat bottom on either
side of legs or wrap arms around legs at the ankles with face down
in their lap.

-CONFIGURE YOUR AIRCRAFT:
High wing aircraft should generally be ditched with full flaps depending on your model and manufacturers recommendations to
reduce airspeed. Low wing aircraft should ditch with the flaps re-
tracted to avoid contacting water first and causing the aircraft to
pitch nose down. A low wing flaps down ditching could possibly
tear off the flaps completely, causing damage to the airframe near
rear wing root and allowing for water entry after impact.

In retractable wheeled and amphibious aircraft have gear selected in the up position when ever possible lessening the chance
of upset.

WATER SURFACE CONDITION CONSIDERATIONS

Determine wind velocity and direction. Conventional wisdom is that the swell direction is more important than the wind direction when planning a ditching.

Plan your approach to land along or parallel to the primary swell, not head on into the tops even when having to accept a strong cross wind.

If the crosswind component exceeds half the landing speed, it might be wiser to land into the wind as long as the touchdown can be made in a valley between swells or on the back side of the swell in ocean conditions.

Again, to reduce the chance of a wingtip digging into water, especially in a low wing aircraft it may be advisable to land along the crest of the swell then slide down into the trough.

With smooth surfaces, especially at night depth perception is greatly diminished making it extremely difficult to judge the water surface. For light aircraft descend at roughly 150-200 feet per minute under power, and dead stick at the best rate of descent with a slightly nose high attitude. Larger aircraft with engine out it is recommended to maintain a 10-12 degrees nose up attitude for fixed gear and add roughly 10-20% airspeed above stall speed until contact with the water surface.

For light retractables the same applies except for a 5-8 degrees nose up attitude due to the faster wing designs.

Other considerations time permitting is to fold jackets or place seat cushions between the front seat occupants and the control yokes if installed on both sides.

I think it's obvious, but the slower an airspeed prior to impact the better to lessen the impact, but do not allow the aircraft to stall or catch a wing tip as either would cause loss of control and could be catastrophic.

For pilots during the descent take a life vest out of its plastic bag and stuff it down your shirt or jacket to ensure you have one available once the Egress is complete and you are outside the sub-merged aircraft, dazed and looking for rescue or shore.

Life vests have a light attached which is water activated within seconds when a rubber seal has been removed to allow water to soak the battery plate creating the necessary current.

In the event your aircraft has sunk with your flashlight inside at night and rescue is searching for you in cold water with temperatures promoting hypothermia, it could be the guiding light literally which saves your life.

For the pilots of nose wheel equipped aircraft if it's possible, just before impact slide your feet off the rudder pedals. The reasoning here was proven in our Cessna 150 accident where the pilot suffered a broken ankle when the nose wheel slammed over to one side on impact ejecting the rudder pedal outward.

Now, after all this planning plus thought towards safety and pre-ditching maneuvers, what about once the time comes when you and your passengers are strapped in, upside down in a sinking aircraft with cold water rushing in.

It could possibly be dark as mentioned earlier, and if you are not prepared or untrained your chances of survival are dramatically reduced along with your fellow aviators.

Here we are now upside down submerged in cold water after a very sudden impact stop and unable to communicate or breathe.

Our first reaction is to release the seat belts then bolt out the door and float up to fresh air, and hopefully the safety of dry land which is not always the case.

Unfortunately this natural reaction and human instinct can often get you into deeper trouble by causing disorientation and confusion, making finding a door handle and opening it properly very difficult.

Again the guideline below is to be considered a plan of attack under most conditions, not taking into account injuries or incapacitation from the impact which would limit physical abilities.

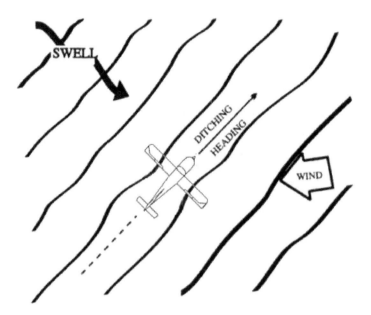

Single Swell (15 knot wind)

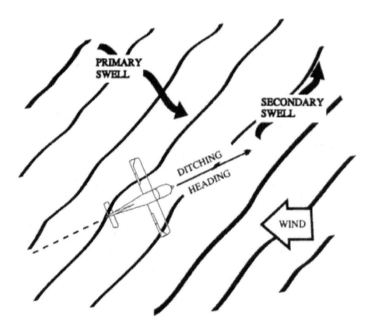

Double Swell (30 knot wind)

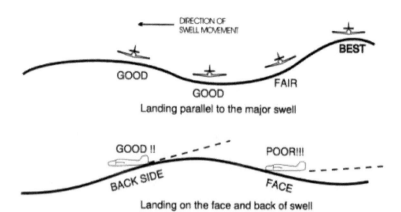

Landing parallel to the major swell

Landing on the face and back of swell

Wind-Swell-Ditch Heading

Wind Speed	Appearance of Sea	Effect on Ditching
0-6 knots	Glassy calm to small ripples	Height very difficult to judge above glassy surface. Ditch parallel to swell
7-10 knots	Small waves; few if any white caps	Ditch parallel to swell
11-21 knots	Larger waves with many white caps	Use headwind component but still ditch along general line of swell
22-33 knots	Medium to large waves, some foam crests, numerous white caps	Ditch into wind on crest or down slope of swell
34 knots and above	Large waves, streaks of foam, wave crests forming spindrift	Ditch into wind on crest or down slope of swell. Avoid at all costs ditching into face of rising swell

Note: The effects on ditching mentioned in the table are appropriate for light aircraft only

POST IMPACT EGRESS

SITUATION 1

AIR POCKET AVAILABLE INSIDE INVERTED FUSELAGE

CREW RESPONSE:
Place your hand on door or exit handle and do not let go remembering the direction of latch travel. If possible converse with passengers as to the plan for escape and have everyone release their belts.

An inverted aircraft even on the surface will have resistance to opening a door, thus you may have to open a window first speeding up the flood of water that will replace the air. Kicking out a jammed door or window, if at all possible would be easier while there is air and vision available prior to a complete submersion.

Once the Egress plan is decided open the door with your hand already on the handle and push outwards allowing water to rush in and have the others follow your lead out of the aircraft.

In the event your door is jammed solid try other exits or use the fire extinguisher bottle to smash a window large enough for all to escape.

Kicking out a window underwater is extremely difficult but if it is the only way out put your back against something solid and make it count, as the exertion will diminish your remaining air.

Depending on your aircraft type being high or low wing, and number of doors this procedure will vary so use it accordingly.

SITUATION 2

INVERTED AIRCRAFT FUSELAGE COMPLETELY FLOODED

CREW RESPONSES:
Stay belted in your seat upside down, then reach over to the door or exit handle and open normally if it's not already ejected.

Once the door is opened grab onto the door frame or anything solid with that same hand, and with your other hand release your seat belts.

With your one hand still holding the door frame pull yourself out head first through the opening and to the surface, eliminating any possibility of disorientation or ending up inside the back of your aircraft.

In the event doors are jammed consider opening any window large enough for your escape or as a last resort pick a suitable sealed window and hope you are able to remove it via brute strength. The best method again is to place your back against something solid and push with all your might using the bottoms of your shoes and strength in your knees. Now back on the surface and after receiving a much needed breath of air, start counting heads bobbing up around you before assessing your next move.

Once all are accounted for inflate your life vests and either start swimming together for land or rescue support equipment. If there are none available, consider staying with your somewhat devalued investment if that looks most promising.

In the event all are not accounted for, only you can make the decision to return for missing passengers and or crew. The perils are endless when rescuing others, given the possibility of an aircraft sinking while you're assisting panicked persons inside who are now very powerful and thus dangerous, or yourself becoming stuck or injured.

Only you will be able to assess the risk for rescuing others given the particular situation, so act accordingly and weigh out the options wisely.

A ditched wheeled aircraft will most likely sink in short order once the wings fill with water depending mostly on the severity of the impact and amount of damage. Inverted seaplanes however could float indefinitely if the actual float compartments were not damaged. Again, given your options regarding distance water temperatures and winds, it could be advisable to sit on a float bottom rather then attempt swimming great distances in chilly water.

Attending our ditch training program at Aviation Egress Systems best follows up what has been discussed here. In actual aircraft inversions most people have some degree of difficulty Egressing in general, and the majority of persons involved go into total panic within 15 seconds when unable to successfully locate an exit. Once an underwater challenge is encountered for the first time high anxiety sets in leading to panic, then the person becomes disorientated leading to inefficiency and could possibly suffer drowning needlessly.

Actual first hand experience in pool simulation teaches the candidate what effects inversion and confinement have on you, and how to react in a positive manner when seconds count towards survival.

At this point I should also mention helicopter ditching behavior as we do train a percentage of rotary wing pilots and passengers. There are distinct differences between fixed wing and helicopters when either one is involved in a ditching, as they both are designed for flight utilizing unique lifting surfaces.

Referring only to the actual water impact while ditching, and what statistically happens shortly after proves the two aircraft are not comparable and must be dealt with accordingly.

When a fixed wing machine on wheels sets up for a landing on any surface with flaps down and a forward gliding speed of normally 60 knots or higher, there will be a sudden stop once contact with the water is made.

There is also the possibility of cartwheeling in the event either wing makes contact first, but often a quick flip over on the aircrafts back is the normal reaction to a ditching situation.

Helicopters with skid style landing gear forced to glide in as per the same scenario even with a powerplant failure are able to auto rotate with a steeper glide rate, but with little or no forward speed once at the water surface.

When any of the external rotors make contact with the water surface they depart rapidly creating a top heavy center of gravity, forcing the machine to roll sideways and inverting thus submerging the entire airframe immediately.

Naturally in either type of unit, be it fixed wing or helicopter they could be subjected to many different impact possibilities being day or night and should be addressed accordingly during training.

Similar to water skiing reading up on any subject is a great start, but the only way to learn this program is by getting wet and taking some spills.

Aviation Egress Systems of Victoria, BC
Founder/instructor Bryan Webster operating
SWET Chair (Shallow Water Egress Trainer)

250-704-6401
www.dunkyou.com
info@dunkyou.com

SWET Chair inversions disorientate students teaching them how to remain calm in a crash simulation. This unit aids instructors in teaching both fixed wing and helicopter ditching.

Willie Burrows aquatic Egress Instructor, assisting with training since conception of **Aviation Egress Systems** in 1998.

The Egress Training Tunnel resembling an inverted aircraft allowing for multiple door and window removals during the training.

CHAPTER THREE

Life Jackets and Personal Floatation Devices

The one most valuable life saving device if you find yourself and possibly others floating in the middle of a lake after your aircraft has sunk could be your PFD. (Personal floatation device)

In the event it was left behind and went down with the ship or failed to inflate properly due to lack of maintenance it could be a major problem not just for you but also your passengers, especially non-swimmers.

First let's look at what you should carry on board the aircraft no matter what configuration and then see if you are properly equipped to take the flight.

If your commercially registered aircraft is on wheels and you are departing for a trip out over a body of water and your enroute portion of flight exceeds your ability to glide to shore, then you are required to supply yourself and each passenger with a Transport Canada/FAA approved PFD. Details found in CAR's # 602.62

Privately registered aircraft in that same scenario again must have floatation devices for each person, but the device is not necessarily under the same approval guidelines and could even be a floatable seat cushion.

In private float equipped aircraft Transport Canada FAA requires each and every seat also to be accompanied by a floatation device for all occupants on any given flight.

How you read the privately registered aircraft regulations will determine what style and model is right for you, but exiting the upside down aircraft could prove if you chose wisely.

The most common unit is the C-13, and has been around for as long as I can remember due to the low cost and availability for an approved inflatable PFD.

Commercial operators on floats are bound by Transport Canada regulations and the FAA to carry at all times and maintain these units for each SOB on an annual basis. In privately owned aircraft however regulations differ and many carry older units that could fail when needed most.

For example, let's say a Cessna 185 was purchased in 1981 on floats and came with a full complement of C-13 PFD's, all brand new and in the sealed plastic bags.

Then in 1988 it was sold and again went with those, now 7 year old life vests which had been tucked away in seat backs and subjected to possible pen punctures and a variety of abuses.

The new owner is happy to see the vests supplied for all his friends and family and ignores their condition plus re-certification due date and carries on for the next 5 years when he/she upgrades to a De Havilland Beaver.

Knowing there are more seats in the Beaver anyway why not buy new ones? The PFD's are left behind for the most recent 185 owner, who is happy with the existing equipment and merrily carries on believing all is well.

These original vests are now 12 years old and have been under fishing tackle boxes and numerous other loads with little regard for their condition and lack of certification ready to go again for another number of years, until someone clues in.

When they are sent out for certification the individual may be surprised to hear they all failed the test and must be replaced due to low Co_2 bottle pressure and deteriorated inflation bags.

This news believe it or not is a good thing, as the worst time to find out there is no parachute in the pack is when you are out the door and free falling to earth.

The Co_2 bottles lose their potency over the years, even when sealed tightly in those plastics bags they came in and the yellow material the inflation bags are made of will not hold air even with a small hole.

You may not even be aware that there are oral inflation tubes in the event the Co_2's fail, but I can assure you most passengers are totally unfamiliar with any safety equipment, especially ones sealed in a pouch.

Transport Canada/ FAA approved C-13 life vest training at
Victoria BC with Aviation Egress Systems.

Students demonstrating the snake maneuver.

Eight person life raft training to demonstrate difficulties
associated with raft entry.

If you elect as a private pilot and owner to go with a boater type floatation device or floating seat cushion, be aware that the floatation of any object inside an aircraft can cause more trouble than good.

Inside an inverted fuselage objects which float become hazards and not only get in the path of your escape but also could possibly entangle you with straps and ties that many have attached to them.

Trying to get anything that produces floatation out of an inverted aircraft can be near impossible, especially when time is limited and others are trying to escape via the same door.

The very worst possible thing you can do on this subject is have anyone on board wearing a floater coat or any style of life vest which has floatation, that includes devices which inflate once immersed in water.

When a child is belted in the back seat of an aircraft wearing a boater style PFD the unit provides roughly 35 lbs lift in water, and then the aircraft is inverted. Not only is the child pinned to the ceiling of that flooded fuselage but the person attempting to rescue will have great difficulty getting them out past the seatbacks etc.

This is why the inflatable life saving equipment was originally designed and tested, thus making it possible for Transport Canada FAA approvals and legal to carry in flight.

The best option is to be wearing your inflatable PFD but the C-13 would not build confidence in your passengers so you may want to research the availability of more socially acceptable units, which are available from a variety of vendors. In some cases, such as an engine failure in flight there may be time available for passengers to don their life vests when a ditching is imminent. Be certain if this plan of action is carried out that you ensure the waist strap is done up tightly around the wearer's waist, and that the tail of the strap is wrapped around the strap itself or tucked into a pocket. This way it cannot become lodged or tangled restricting anyone's Egress after an impact. Be extremely careful as well that in the event seat belts were removed in this procedure, that the belt was done up snugly afterwards and the release mechanism is facing outwards. For us pilot types in flight there is little chance of controlling the aircraft, deciding where to ditch plus talking to both passengers and anyone who will listen to our plight on the radio, so as mentioned earlier I simply suggest stuffing the PFD in your shirt or jacket as it will be available to you once bobbing on the surface.

The actual donning of the C-13 PFD is simple. Open your pouch then find the only hole and put your head through it as there is no upside down or backwards.

Once you are wearing the unit and not planning to return to the flooded aircraft for any reason find the 2 red plastic pull-tabs and jerk downward releasing the compressed air contained in the Co_2 bottles, which will then immediately fill the floatation bags giving you the ability to float without having to swim.

About this time you will want to do up the waist strap, which may be found hanging freely somewhere around your mid section. Failure to do so is uncomfortable and makes it awkward to move about in the water.

Now depending on your situation, a decision has to be made regarding staying with a half submerged airframe which may be your best bet or attempting to swim for dry land.

I recall stories from old timers in the Canadian north where after a float aircraft ditched thus more than one pilot and passenger sat patiently waiting for the wind to blow them in the direction of shore, while perched soaking wet on the float bottoms. In one case there was an off shore north wind from the upset site and the two unfortunate individuals floated clear across a large lake right through the night to reach the south shore, only to have a days walk back to their original landing site. They stated that it was a better option than a swim in the ice cold water even though the original distance was negligible. One of them was a non-swimmer but PFD's were unheard of in those years. Some of the challenges you may want to consider before making your decision to stay with your ship or swim from a ditching providing your craft appears to remain afloat are;

-Water temperature
-Degree of Hypothermia
-Wind speed
-Injuries
-Swimming capabilities
-PFD's or the lack there of
-Search and rescue response time
-Location of closest support or aid
-Distance of proposed float or swim
-In warm water shark concerns
-Time of day regarding warmth
-Taking a vote from all involved

Other safety items attached to your C-13 are a water actuated light that may come in handy after dark for rescue, and a whistle. In cold water either one of these items could speed up a rescue when hypothermia is lurking only minutes away, and the cold water is cooling your body core 27 times faster than same air temperature.

The light should be on moments after submersion in any liquid but if not find the blue battery pack and remove the orange tab marked with something like "pull here" depending on the manufacturer.

The whistle will not only assist in rescue as its sound travels further including over the noise of outboard motors, but also sealing your lips around it keeps water from being swallowed every time you open your mouth and call HELP.

The decision to swim especially in a group has a few things to be aware of in helping extend your ability to make that elusive island off in the distance, providing all involved are wearing some kind of life jacket.

Travel in a line known as the snake maneuver where the leader lies on their back and the next person lies against them, also on their back locking the forward person with their legs around the next person's waist. Continue this procedure until everyone is in line and locked together. Then paddle in unison utilizing your hands as the oars providing any injuries from the impact allow for this.

When great distances exceed possible limits for swimming to

safety, or injuries prevent travel and the airframe has recently become a diver's reef, circle together and lock arms at your elbows then stay as close together as possible.

The PFD will do the work in keeping you on the surface so now it is important to conserve your body core temperature by using each other's bodies to insulate the immediate water surrounding each other.

In the event there are any floating objects including the plastic bag your C-13 came in, place it on your head to slow the cooling process. This being the only part of your body above water surface and it expels huge amounts of body heat.

For injured or incapacitated persons circle to form a human floating gurney and keep their head above water with them in the middle, allowing the PFD to do the work and the bodies to warm each other.

In some cases such as rough seas, it may be advantageous to hold each other in a group by snapping one another's waist belts together, or by tying waist belts in the event the snaps are non compatible.

The best way for you to practice life vest training is to try one on in a pool and blowing it up, or if you take any kind of Egress course this should be part of the program.

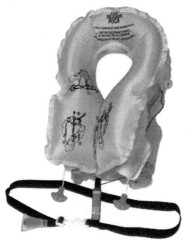

Featuring:

➤ FAA-TSO C13d, C13e, C13f Approved
➤ Double Cells for added safety
➤ Flame resistant urethane coated nylon
➤ Heat-sealed seams
➤ FAA-TSO C85 approved water activated
   Locator Light
➤ Dual oral tubes
➤ Easy to identify international yellow in color
All Provided as Standard Equipment

Options Available:

➤ Police Whistle
➤ Mirror
➤ Sea Dye Marker
➤ Multi-lingual pull tab instructions
➤ Customized donning instructions
➤ Airline Logo
➤ Varied bags and packing configurations
➤ Differentiating orange crew vests available
➤ Demo vests available for inflight safety
   instructions
➤ 16 gm CO_2 Replacement Cylinders available

Example of aviation style C 13 life vest

Cessna 185 sinking while taxiing prior to take off due to loss of float ball seals and a heavy load allowing water to enter at the rear of the float.

Pilot attempting to beach aircraft by adding power.

Pilot shut down engine and assess situation.

Now it appears sinking is imminent thus pilot and passenger evacuate and wait for a boat which is on the way. Both occupants and aircraft are rescued by a local boat operator. Luckily there was no damage and the aircraft was supported before being towed to shore.

Pictures supplied by Gary McLeod of Vancouver BC taken in 1989 at Stony Rapids Saskatchewan.

CHAPTER FOUR

Amphibious Aircraft

The beauty of amphibious aircraft is the versatility gained when you are given the option of taking off and landing on runways or water.

In the morning you may wander down to the beach in front of your cottage, hop in your aircraft and taxi out on the lake, take off to a destination where there is a paved runway and taxiway right into the convenience of a covered hangar out of the weather.

For the loss of a seat or possibly two due to the weight of tire/ brake assemblies and hydraulic pumps etc, you may have floats installed with the added feature of these extendable wheels.

There are amphibs installed on aircraft such as ultra- lights and Piper Super Cubs right through most of the Cessna series and De Havilland products, not to mention hundreds of other aircraft models including home builts.

Then of course there are flying boats where the fuselage bottom is the main structure of the craft designed as a boat hull with wings attached, main wheels are tucked up tightly mid ship with a tail wheel at the rear hidden away until required. No matter the configuration in all of these machines you will find freedom only multi task aircraft are able to provide, and which operate both privately and commercially all over the world.

For the pilot there is no major conversion from floats to a set of amphibs, but it is recommended you receive a thorough check out from a person who has experience on your specific aircraft configuration.

There are a few things to be aware of, especially if you have flown your aircraft for a number of years on the same set of standard floats. All amphibs should come complete with a gear position-warning device, exceptions being the ultra-light series of air-craft due to limited electrical system and weight concerns.

This addition to your dash indicator works the same way as any retractable, with an up/down selector handle and series of lights. With three of each color for tail wheeled flying boats or four of each color for standard floats, which are commonly blue for water and brown or green for land.

As a routine, when doing your walk around on land it is a good idea to check that the gear switch is in the down position prior to turning on the master switch, even though there may be squat switches protecting an inadvertent gear up condition. At the same time unlock all your doors and exits including cargo doors giving others more options to rescue you in the unlikely event that one day you are upside down filling with water right in front of your favorite marina. Due to the aircraft all up weight many amphibs will have two main wheels under each mid float section, but they are still indicated with one light for that wheel position.

These systems are normally driven by a hydraulic pump located in one of the float compartments, and backed up by a mechanical hand pump and handle located on the dash or floor within easy reach of the pilot's seat.

Things you will find different when converting to an amphib are firstly the aircraft is heavier with the extra gear and equipment involved for this configuration, thus it will extend your water or ground run from both liquid or off a hard surface. When taxiing to the active runway in a conventional floatplane amphib there are no nose wheel brakes and the 2 front tires are normally free castering, thus it takes a while to become comfortable getting around the airport aprons and taxiway lights.

On take off from a runway surface with amphibious floats the aircraft is now sitting flat on 4 tire locations giving a feeling of solid stability until you build speed and raise the nose freeing the front wheels from the ground.

About this time, especially if there is any crosswind you may feel strangely uncomfortable as the aircraft is lifting off due to the rigid gear and lack of side play normally provided on spring or leaf style gear legs.

After take off from a runway surface especially in the event you are immediately out over water select gear up once you see a positive rate of climb, and continue the flight with gear up until required for a future hard surface landing. Although there is less parasite drag from these wheel extensions versus a retractable wheeled aircraft it is still advisable to get the gear up soon as practical after take off from a runway indicated by the blue lights being illuminated. When departing from a water surface the lift off will be normal thus the gear will stay in the up position until there is a runway landing required.

Your POH will explain the gear systems in detail including the lights and gear selector. In particular study the emergency gear extension procedure and what to do in the event a pump motor fails, trips a breaker or bursts a hydraulic line. Whenever possible after salt water operations it is advisable to cycle the gear down and up in a fresh water lake while taxiing at idle speed to flush out the wheel wells and associated parts.

The same idle speed rule applies for lowering the gear after landing on water with intentions for beaching or taxing up a slipway to avoid over stressing the front gear legs.

The most important information I can possibly pass on to you regarding any type of amphibious aircraft is the unforgiving mistake of landing with the gear selected down on water, or the opposite somewhat less dramatic landing with gear selected up on a runway.

Gear down water landings most often flip the aircraft and unsuspecting pilot/ passengers with a violent and sudden stop inverted, followed by an equally traumatic Egress situation you will wish had never happened.

The opposite condition of landing gear up on the runway normally proves less exciting and more upright but very embarrassing, and it can be expensive to repair the damaged float bottoms particularly on a gravel strip.

This situation happens on a regular basis and can almost always be directed towards pilot error, which is why insurance companies increase your hull coverage rates the moment they hear the word amphibious.

So why does this continue to happen with gear mirrors, mechanical indicators and all our new technologies involving multiple warning horns and audible safety device advancements?

Simply put, to err is to be human and there is no fool proof guarantee to date that landing in the proper configuration is assured, thus we must be diligent by backing up voice commands and horns with a simple check list. The problem occurs when you take off from a lake in the morning and fly to an airport thus gear down, then off to the ocean and gear up, now another lake then river and on to eight more different destinations before heading to home base just before dark. On a two mile final with gear down to land and hangar for the night a guy ahead of you bounces hard and veers off the runway with a cloud of dust and a blown left main tire changing your intentions to land as planned. Being the resourceful pilot that you are and simply wanting to get home we overshoot and elect to line up with that familiar floatplane base right next to our runway and guess what, an unexpected swim before dinner. To combat this scenario my personal suggestion is to make a check list printed back to back on the same laminated piece of paper, colored blue on one side for floats and brown or what ever color matches your gear lights on the other side for hard surface landings. By getting into the habit of selecting the gear for the proposed landing and visually looking at the landing site, then confirming for example a blue lake with the same color gear lights and checklist you can be certain things are in order even when fatigue or complacency enters the equation. The hard core realities are that if there were 10 floatplanes all operating from one base for 20 years and only one was amphibious, if any one aircraft were to succumb to an upset the most likely candidate would be the one with the option of wearing wheels.

Cessna 208 Grand Caravan
Ferried from Zurich Switzerland to Dubai UAE October 2001 by Bryan
Webster

24 hour stop over at Barain UAE

CHAPTER FIVE

Ski Planes and What To Watch For

Are you are presently thinking "why would I take any interest in ski planes"? If this is the case more than likely you live south of the 49th Parallel and have little if any interest in visiting Northern Canada or Alaska any time soon.

What has snow and ice got to do with ditching aircraft anyways? Well read on if for nothing else than to maybe understand and appreciate the challenges associated with operating in sub zero temperatures.

To pilots and passengers who commute from Northern communities to far off destinations year round where roads are often either impassable or non-existent at times, a set of skis where the floats were once attached is invaluable. These brave individuals in aviation wake up extra early each day to deal with the cold temperatures, bone chilling winds and ice conditions that often make you wonder why anyone would consider such a task. Since the early days of flight these people have faced the elements and hardships in opening up the far reaches of North America to mining exploration and bring much needed supplies for many small villages in remote locations.

From the 1930's through to today not all that much has changed for ski operators, with the exception of newer technologies and advancements making a difficult situation more manageable.

The original pioneers quickly learnt all about the problems with cold engine starting and having to drain the crankcase oil every evening, then sharing quarters with the stuff all night while it hopefully remained in a liquid state on a wood stove.

In the morning they would stumble in the direction of a snow covered aircraft with a canvas tent draped over the nose cowl and light a temperamental fuel/oil heater, which on occasion caught fire and burnt the entire aircraft beyond recognition.

After pouring the oil back into the engine and going through all the numerous steps of readying their craft for flight they then were faced with standing out at –30 Celsius with the wind howling and hand prop the engine while standing in waist deep snow.

Today we are fortunate in having things like insulated Velcro wrapped nose covers and block or fan heaters, which plug into the lightweight portable generator and warms not only the engine but also battery and cockpit whenever away from base.

Just remember though, if the generator refuses to start then once again just as in the old days you will be forced to seek out ingenious ways of heating your craft possibly located many miles from anything. As I said earlier things have not really changed all that much.

Aircraft reliability and cabin warmth in flight have advanced significantly, especially the turbine-equipped machines which are not as critical when it comes to cold weather starts.

Today sturdy aluminum construction and Teflon bottoms have replaced the old style wood skis that were often susceptible to cracking and sticking to the snow surface.

Another great improvement is the wheel/ski which was designed for allowing the take off on a hard surface runway and later landing on a snow or ice surface by means of lowering the skis and having the tires rest on their top surface.

Again, use of a check list is suggested as it can be quite expensive when landing on a bare and dry paved runway after returning from a trip north involving an ice strip, and forgetting the skis in the down position.

The actual training for skis is not much different from normal wheel landings once you become familiar with the snow surface and wallowing effect skis and external bungees bring with them.

Depending on your flight environment and snow conditions knowing where to land is the trick, as in the far north many aircraft have lost gear legs landing into large, unpredictable wind drifted surfaces as hard as cement.

When you go to purchase insurance for that winter friendly addition to your aircraft there may be a requirement to build time with an already ski familiar pilot for a minimum number of hours.

Now that you are all checked out and flying merrily around the frozen landscape, always be prepared to spend a night out in the bush in the event weather closes in at the other end, or when starting with a cold battery becomes a problem.

Always being prepared with heavy jackets, gloves and boots plus all the other winter temperature paraphernalia is mandatory, including that of your passengers who will become your problem in the event they were not well outfitted.

Survival kits already include matches and food plus many useful items for wilderness stays, but sleeping bags and axes should be also onboard when warranted for winter survival in severe cold situations.

The next topic to discuss here is ice conditions and thickness, which is why you find this information in a book on aircraft ditching in the first place.

When landing on a lake or any body of water covered with ice there is no guarantee until you are stopped and drill a hole for measuring thickness, that you and your craft are located on a solid surface.

Many aircraft and a wide variety of equipment in general all over the north have found out the hard way when ice thickness was insufficient or rotten and unable to support the object.

The serious side of this situation for pilots and their shocked ski plane passengers immediately after falling through to their wings, is the frigid water pouring in flooding their craft and the immediate realization of being trapped inside by the very ice they are resting on.

In many incidents such as this the occupants were forced to kick out front windows or chop their way through the cabin ceiling with an axe, or use of a knife in the fabric-covered machines due to ice jamming side doors closed.

Facts of winter and operating in the far north are simple, in sub zero temperatures if your clothing gets soaked through there is potential for severe frostbite or even loss of life if warmth is not found soon after.

Hypothermia will set in only a few minutes later after a dunking in ice cold water if you end up submerged, and have no ability of finding shelter close by or any heat source.

There are charts available for knowing the amount of ice required to safely support your aircraft, but remember where there is moving water below the ice its thickness could be considerably thinner.

From the Egress point of view always look around the aircraft you are about to take flying, and imagine yourself having to find a way out if all doors are secured against the ice surface on the outside after falling straight through.

Do you have the ability to get out, and is there adequate equipment to aid in your escape? If not, seriously consider the scenario you and your passengers may find yourselves in and act accordingly.

Cessna 185 on skis fallen through rotten spring ice

Cessna 185 Bryan Webster North of Fort Smith NWT 1986

CHAPTER SIX

Lake Lovely Water Adventure

It was the spring of 1959 and a warm clear blue morning when a young couple planned a flight into their favorite mountain lake for the day. Their aircraft a Piper 20 which is a basic Tri Pacer on floats was waiting for them at a local Vancouver BC area airport a short distance from their home.

They arrived at the field and met up with their female friend who also enjoyed flying and the idea of helping open up their alpine hiking club's small cabin tucked away at a remote destination. They loaded their supplies in the four seat Piper which was predominately used as a logging company supply transporter for men and equipment to camps up and down the BC Coast.

The proposed flight was less than an hour from home base and they departed from sea level in their craft and climbed North West to the Coast Mountains where their picturesque remote lake awaited them above 3000 feet.

On arrival the trio circled the small lake tucked away in the backdrop beauty of the glaciers and huge peaks melting the winter's snow into creeks and meadows below.

The landing was uneventful and soon after they were prying off the plywood bear covers from the windows and readying the quaint base camp building for yet another summer of alpine wilderness adventure.

For a short while the three enjoyed the fresh air and admired the landscape, realizing how fortunate they were to be able to experience the grandeur of the serenity offered at this location.

With the building aired out after a winter of cold and snow, they enjoyed an outdoor lunch on the shore of the pristine waters below the camp and discussed the wonders of flight and how long it may have taken to hike into this location.

Soon the urge to hook a few trout at nearby Garibaldi Lake became the focus, so they now prepared for a departure from their high altitude Lake Lovely Water to the next venue of the day before returning home. Knowing the P-A20 had weight limitations with the low horsepower, and short water run available plus thinner air it was decided their friend would wait on the shore for the second trip to lighten the load.

With the engine started the propeller pulled the little craft to the far end of the lake giving as much room as possible for the water run required for the vertical distance to clear the solid granite which surrounded their picture perfect paradise.

Shortly after lift off and nearing the end of the lake disaster struck. The little plane was climbing normally when an unexpected shift in winds followed by descending air slammed them hard back onto the water drowning the engine and heavily damaging the floats.

The airframe and one wing slowly began to lean to the side listing dramatically, to a point where it was obvious they would roll over and must vacate their craft immediately.

This particular aircraft was designed with the only door available located on the right side, thus our passenger quickly departed out followed by the pilot as the poor craft leaned precariously.

Then as the pair climbed to higher ground the aircraft began to roll upside down leaving them to clutch onto the damaged undercarriage and assess their situation.

Moments later their predicament got worse as the aircraft sunk and left them roughly 1500 feet from shore submersed in the icy cold spring water and wondering what had just happened.

To add yet another challenge, the passenger was a total non-swimmer and would have drowned right there and then if not for the strength and persistence of her husband. During the short swim to shore they were suffering from sore and cramping muscles while hypothermia set in, making it difficult to breathe and continue on to safety.

Once on shore and nearly exhausted they stripped down and draped their soaked cloths over the smooth rocks which were plentiful, and took advantage of the warm spring sun until everything was dry enough to wear once again. By this time their friend who had witnessed the mishap arrived from her journey on foot from the opposite side of the lake. Being as the aircraft was submerged in water and this happening long before aviation style ELT's were invented, a swift and timely rescue was out of the question.

Without any emergency kit or food supplies they decided that descending the mountain to the nearby village of Squamish would be the most suitable option.

Estimations were made for the time it would take but the best guess was if they left immediately and hiked until dark, tomorrow afternoon would find them at a local hotel for lunch and a warm shower. For the remainder of that day the trio compared the ease of air travel to the harsh bush and terrain offered by the coastal undergrowth of British Columbia.

Finally just before dark they came across a wide flowing river at the base of the mountain they had successfully descended.

Tired and hungry not to mention the painful swollen feet from inappropriate footwear, they made camp under an overhang on the river shore.

Just as they were settling for the night a pair of hunters arrived on the opposite shore in hopes of being the early birds that bag the moose in the morning when hunting season opened. After a series of hand signals and attempts at yelling over the sound of the rapids, the point was made this was not a planned overnight in the wilds for our downed aviators.

After darkness set in the would be hunters traversed the river in an inflatable raft borrowed from a nearby forestry camp which they had passed earlier in the day on the way out from town and paddled to the trio's rescue.

Before long they were being driven back to town in a pickup truck saving the next day's long uncomfortable trek and enjoyed the night indoors at the Squamish Hilton.

Early the next morning they caught a train which transported them back to Vancouver where they filled out the necessary paperwork on the mishap that left the little aircraft in 300 feet of water, and which stayed there for the next 39 years.

In 1999 I rescued the PA-20 airframe mentioned in this story after it had been stripped of the engine and was on route to the local landfill. That engine unbelievably was rebuilt, mainly due to the cold acid free water and was then installed into a homebuilt aircraft that same year.

I returned a few keepsake items found in the glove box such as pens and a knife, to the passenger who was sitting in the right front seat when the crash occurred, and she shared with me this entire story in great detail.

Bryan Webster

PA-20 Floatplane ditched at Lake Lovely Water in 1959 and retrieved in
the late 1980's from a depth of 300 feet

CHAPTER SEVEN

Real Life Stories

Martin Hale from Whitefish Montana USA writes-

I started flying with a private license (SEL) in 1980, then two years later received a float rating which was one of my life's biggest thrills. Today I fly my Cessna 180 modified with a 0-520 and three bladed propeller on floats.

My flight time exceeds 5000 hours with the majority being on those floats that have taken me to places all over North America few people get to see, including Alaska for up to five times annually.

Even with all that past experience I am a long way from knowing it all as flying has numerous challenges and no one person could live long enough to be caught in every scenario.

That is what brought me to Bryan Webster's Aviation Egress Systems pilot and passenger ditching school.

I had no idea what the program was all about, but was keen to learn whatever is offered which will improve my piloting or overall survival skills. The ground school was a real eye opener as everything that was discussed dealt with real life situations that have happened to aviators similar to me.

One quickly realizes how important Egress training could be the first time you are rolled upside down and become totally disoriented and unable to find the door handles inside their ditching simulators.

I absolutely had no idea of the challenges that present themselves in Egressing a flipped over aircraft, or the speed at which they occur. The AES program makes the pilot think of things like different kinds of passengers that are transported in aircraft whether on wheels or floats, and what could happen if one ends up inverted in a lake or river.

Example: What about passengers who are non-swimmers, large or elderly not to mention children who rely totally on us for advice and leadership especially under the stress of an accident.

We were taught first hand how dangerous a boater's style life vest or jacket could be inside an aircraft under water in the simulators, and why inflatable PFD'S were invented for aircraft originally.

You will learn about the options available for life vests and why pilots and passengers should be wearing inflatable units, as even when ready in a warm swimming pool most of us left them behind in the rush to get out.

I have tried to talk many of my aviation buddies to take the time and attend this course with a variety of responses.

One pilot said, "Oh I will just be careful and not take chances". Others were concerned about performing poorly in front of their friends, or were uncomfortable in water.

A person should put the concerns out of his/her mind and sign up soon, especially if are apprehensive as this is all the more reason to attend. Plan to use this opportunity to learn and practice these skills in a safe controlled environment where if you do poorly there are chances to repeat the procedure and get it right the next time.

A floatplane pilot is no more than a log in the water, rogue wave or sudden gust of wind away from a possible upset and one must be prepared for such an event.

I have now taken this course twice, as I realized after my first session that my wife who flies with me on a regular basis should also be proficient in Egressing a ditching as I could be incapacitated during a real incident.

I strongly believe in the Egress training provided, and tell all other pilots you cannot appreciate the benefits until you complete the course.

The one group of pilots who does understand why this is so important are our military folks who have long understood the dangers and repeated this training annually for years as it is mandatory for them.

Just like practicing engine failures and stalls this should be included in any pilot's emergency training program.

Signed Martin Hale.

Martin Hale of Whitefish Montana USA and his Cessna 180

Brenda Matas from Campbell River BC writes-

Several years ago my late husband and I were practicing flying skills in our Super 22 Bushmaster which we had spent many years previous building, and at the time were installed on floats. By the end of that day we were both at the hospital and left with a major aircraft rebuild project once again, plus wondering what had just happened. I was passenger that day sitting beside my husband who was in the left seat of our aircraft while he performed standard step taxi techniques. We had no intention of actually going flying as there was a low ceiling and it was simply to refresh us and blow the dust off our aircraft. We both had pilot licenses and also had been taking helicopter pilot training on a Bell 46. That particular day though we wanted to get back into the fixed wing world once again which is considerably different. Once on the step at a moderate speed we were scooting across the water surface and I was face down immersed in twiddling dials on the Loran.

A moment later the engine sound changed and I felt us lift off, realizing we were in the air I assumed my husband would just land again but this was not the case. We continued to remain airborne and then he initiated a left down wind turn back to base, unfortunately the next thing I knew we were heading straight down on my side as the upper wing had stalled. I remember putting my hands on the seat belt and thinking don't do anything until it stops, at which time water pressure pushed me violently backwards in the seat with such force I was pinned until there was silence.

Amazingly we stopped in an upright position, but there was water flooding the cabin rapidly thus I quickly undid my seat belts and assisted my unconscious husband who had hit his head on the dash.

He soon regained composure and we escaped through the front window just as the aircraft rolled inverted and forced us to take refuge on the one intact float bottom, which was supporting the craft on the water surface.

About that time a paddle and life vest had been collected from debris floating freely about the downed craft, and plans for floating to the nearby shore had been made when a boat appeared in the distance and helped transport us to the local hospital for medical aid.

For me this was the end of the days flying but the beginning of a nightmare that started with agonizing dreams of being trapped underwater and searching in vain for non existent passengers until waking up shaking, sweating and crying. Once the aircraft had been repaired two years later I attempted a recurrence training program with an experienced instructor, but solo flight brought back the post crash anxiety.

At times just the sight of an aircraft gave me anxiety, and I seriously considering giving up flying and selling the aircraft in hopes the situation would improve. Then I heard about Aviation Egress Systems training program and eventually got up the nerve to call them to discuss my options.

I spoke with Bryan Webster and after numerous conversations agreed to attend one of his Egress classes and thus return mentally to the scene of the crime where I had been so deeply affected now several years prior. When I arrived at the pool facility physically shaking and having serious doubts about attending the program Bryan and his staff assured me this was the best therapy, and the training would help alter my path in life that had been so deeply affected since the crash.

After calming down and becoming part of the class discussions on how to handle and think about ditching we reviewed my story, and even the group helped assure me this would be the best way to dispel my fears.

In the pool I was reluctant and viewed the equipment as terrifying, but forced myself to continue and progressed in a methodical manner from basic life vest drills to working underwater opening doors and windows. Only after watching the other students take numerous dunkings in their simulators did I agree to take the plunge and was soon repeating the roll over procedure until the paralyzing fear that gripped me subsided. By the end of the day I was calm and reacting in the appropriate manner that gained the respect of everyone involved, which helped me overcome my past negative experience.

Bryan Webster knew what I did not. He knew from his own experience I had to go back to that underwater experience again and this was why he was so persuasive. I finally worked up the courage to take that course and I am very happy that I did it. Huge progress has been made from the gut wrenching apprehension at every landing, to now having the confidence that I can think my way through any underwater Egress situation. Since that day in 2001 I now sleep well at night and am back flying my Bushmaster all over the country without apprehension and plan to take another AES pilot ditching course again in the future.

Signed - Brenda Matas

Brenda Matas with her Super 22 Bushmaster

Actual aircraft ditching experience

I think it is best to share my experience as hopefully someone else could learn something and possibly not lose his or her life. I have many reservations about telling this, as the trauma (mental) is quite high, but something inside me urges me to pass this on.

It was July 11ᵗʰ 1997 when my wife and I decided we should fly our Cessna 185 to Nimpo Lake in central BC. On our arrival at the lake we met a couple just married spending their honeymoon in a cabin nearby, and who asked if they could ride along with us in our aircraft. We were happy that we could provide a "floatplane" experience to such a cute couple, so off the four of us went.

We flew into Turner Lake, walked around the unbelievable Hunlen Falls, and then back towards the dock to head for the cabins where we were staying a short distance away by air. Prior to our departure my wife explained to the couple that in the event of an emergency landing the first thing to do is remove your seatbelt.

I don't know why she told them that as that is not normally something that my wife thinks about, weird. We were going to take the route down the canyon to fly over Knott Lake and then up the Klinnilinni River to home, but after take off I thought it best to fly over Charlotte Lake as there are immense landing opportunities should an engine failure occur. This is something that I regularly think of when flying as I am always looking for a place to land. So over Charlotte Lake we went, and then flew just off the water at 50 feet to get a view of the abandoned Remarko Ranch.

After the look see I started a steep climb and a banking turn to head home and to gain the much needed altitude. Suddenly, there was a deafening silence……. The engine had quit.

We were at the edge of the lake on the East end right over the camping beach…. which was full of sun worshipers as this was a holiday and such a beautiful day to enjoy the outdoors. With only about 400' of altitude our options were quite limited. Knowing the amount of fuel I had and not wanting to put the plane into the trees for fear of fire, I though it best to try to turn 180 degrees and get back into the wind for an attempt to put down on the water. If I had opted to land straight ahead most likely we would have skidded up onto the beach killing who knows how many. The plane sank fast as we were losing both altitude and speed quickly. When I finally got the plane turned around, we had lost about 390 feet altitude and all of our flying speed. There was a faint hope that I could flare and make a safe landing but with no speed and less altitude remaining the plane stalled, we hit the hard surface of the water from about 10'. This made the front left side of the float dig into the water which immediately flipped the plane on its nose and then over on its back, ripping off the left wing.

The force broke out a portion of the windscreen and immediately after coming to rest inverted we started to fill up with water rapidly. I remember looking over at my wife who had the rear seat passenger on top of her who was bleeding profusely all over her white shirt. He had flown over the front seat and hit his head on the V-brace, then he looked at my wife and said "Don't Panic". What happened next is a horrible blur. I remember trying to get my belt off but hanging upside down didn't help matters. I tried opening up the door…which was jammed as the impact twisted the cabin frame. I tried the seat belt again, this time while underwater to no avail. I lost total recall of what the others were doing. By now I began to wonder if I could hold my breath any longer. Door? Seat Belt? Nothing was working and then I remember a most peaceful feeling that everything was okay. I sat back into my seat and quit struggling as it was all over for me. The last thing I remember about being under water is that somehow in the struggling to get free my elbow must have knocked my side door window open.

I still do not now how I got my seat belt off, I don't remember doing it. But I do remember that when I squeezed out of that tiny side window opening and swam up to the surface how good it felt to take a breath of air. It seemed like a dream, and then I realized that I was the only one on the surface. I knew that the others were still down there inside the wreckage.

I took a deep breath and swam back down to the submerged aircraft roughly 12 feet below where the inverted plane was being supported by the one float, which was still partially attached. I remember with my first attempt I couldn't make it mainly because of the pressure on my ears which was killing me.

I surfaced and took another breath, this time clearing my ears on the way down only to find that I couldn't open the doors to get them out.

I surfaced again took another breath and this time went to the baggage door, which fortunately was unlocked. When I opened that little door I immediately saw the male passenger.

Grabbing on I helped him out the baggage door and we both went to the surface. He was conscious. Again I went down for another attempt this time for his wife. I went through the same struggle to get her out the baggage door.

Realize the door is only about 12 x 15 inches. When we surfaced a boat approached to help in the rescue with a fisherman on board. Helping the couple into the boat took all of my attention, and then I realized that my wife was still down there in the plane. So I quickly dove back down again and got inside to pull her out of her seatbelt and managed to get her through the door and to the surface. She had swallowed a lot of water and was not coherent. The people on the boat pulled her in and I remember how she coughed up a "ton" of water when they pulled her across the side of the boat forcing it out.

I know someone was watching out for me that day, as there are many happenings that were too much coincidence. Lessons to learn? Both my wife and I were wearing shoulder harnesses; this saved our lives as the force had thrown us forward into the full extension of those belts. My wife had black and blue marks across her chest from the waist to her shoulders from where she hit the belt. Had we not been wearing them, she and I would have definitely hit the instrument panel and been knocked out and we would have drowned. Another miracle...I always keep the baggage door locked as my small children ride in the 3rd seat in the back of the plane. Why was it unlocked that day I will never know.

Still...had we chosen to go down over Knott Lake instead, we would have had no witnesses to our accident, and for the man in the boat being there to pull us in saved our lives. I remember how hard it was swimming just the 10 feet in my clothes, especially with shoes on. Still another...how...did the window pop open. And how did we all get out of our seatbelts? I do not remember.

Looking back, there are things that I would have done differently and which I do now every time I take someone for a ride...I explain the urgency to get the seatbelts off. I would try to open the door prior to impact, and most assuredly, I would make sure that those in the front seat wear shoulder harnesses. The disorientation that set in once we were upside down and under water was indescribable. I couldn't find my door handle for the longest time, I couldn't even efficiently find the release latch for the seatbelt.

Practicing and locating these two things in advance could really save your life.

After we got the plane out of the water and during recovery, we found there to be 26 gallons of fuel. Both main door inside handles had been turned so hard that the spines on the shaft had been twisted clear off the door handle, so opening the door would have been impossible from the inside. I guess in our panic, we unknowingly had tried so hard that we just ripped the handles off.

I hope this has provided some helpful tips.

Anonymous

CHAPTER EIGHT

Bry the Dunker Guy Cessna 150 Ditching Story

At the end of chapter one I finished with yours truly onboard a Cessna 150 then hitting the mighty Fraser River at high speed while attempting to avoid a newly installed set of power lines which lay across our flight path.

At the time I was 17 and had 35 hours Total Time and a whole lot more to learn about my aviation career, but this was a great beginning lesson.

Needless to say we should have not been down so low especially flying into a setting sun on an August evening that would have avoided this entire mishap, but hindsight is always 20-20.

During impact I clearly recall the front widow ejecting and an incredible force of water ramming into our faces, then I felt the nose wheel assembly smash the belly skins right underneath my seat.

After that I only recall silence, until moments later when I awoke to an eerie lack of engine noise and a cold sensation on my forehead which was continuing to progress downwards to my eyebrows.

I shook my head and realized we had just crashed and we were rapidly sinking into the dirty brown silty waters of the same river that only moments before we were merrily cruising above.

Looking to my left there was my blood soaked buddy hanging lifeless in his harnesses about to slide silently underwater as the stricken aircraft headed for the rivers bottom.

Realizing our predicament I unbuckled my harness and attempted to bail out the open door only to find my left ankle firmly attached via a heavy mike coily cord which had wound around my leg several times and was securely affixed to the under dash by the plug in end.

Returning into the sinking ship once again I searched underwater for the jack plug in site under the dash and pulled down on the cable releasing me from the trap.

Now free and unrestricted I floated around the rear of the aircraft and over to the pilot's side door which was luckily also wide open due to the water's impact force's ejecting through the front window on impact.

Reaching in underwater I located his seat belt release and pulled, he literally floated out into my arms with the aid of a 5-knot river current. At this time only the belly of the aircraft and gear legs with wheels attached were exposed, thus I held the still unconscious captains head above water while balancing on a wing strut until literally the aircraft sank and disappeared out of sight.

Just about then while doing the back float in the direction of shore my lifeless accomplice regained consciousness and blurted out "what has happened and where is my aircraft".

I replied 'it is on the bottom and we have just crashed so lets get to shore' which with the current would be a fair journey to say the least.

Luckily there was a pair of riverbank fishermen enjoying the afternoon from lawn chairs. They were witness to our performance right in front of them and later offered aid in our safe return to dry land.

On our swim into shore roughly half way from the crash site, a fellow hollered out to us that his buddy was on the way to a local farmhouse in search of a telephone regarding our obvious need of an ambulance.

Soon after I bumped the bottom while doing the backstroke and realized we were now in shallow water and stood up to walk the remainder distance to shore.

Once we were on our feet though my flying buddy found out his forehead wound was not the only post crash problem associated with the incident, as it turned out he also had a broken ankle.

Right about then I was snagged securely by a fishhook and literally reeled in by the lone fisherman who then pulled out a knife and managed to cut my pants free of the hook, plus a sizeable chunk of his own flesh adding to the blood flow situation involving my buddy's head.

While dealing with his own finger laceration he was kind enough to offer their lawn chairs and a blanket, which was much appreciated as our Captain was in need of both moral and medical support.

Then seeing some of our aircraft wreckage parts floating away downstream I dove back in and rounded up an assortment of nose-wheel and cowl parts to save for whatever reason. They eventually ended up being only souvenirs and the entire wreckage was sold for pennies per pound.

From the distance an approaching siren grew louder and soon we were surrounded by medical personnel attending to my buddy's needs and asking me what hurts, and had happened.

My ailments were very minor in comparison to his, mine consisted of facial and chest/neck bruising where you could plainly see the shoulder harness webbing imprints.

Then off we went to the local hospital, and within a few hours found ourselves standing on the front steps discussing the day's events while awaiting a ride back home.

The next day I flew my 150 back over the site taking pictures and trying to reassemble the why's and what if's which you find yourself pondering after such happenings.

I was surprised to find the 16 wires totally unmarked, but even more shocked to see that the steel towers on either side of the river were completely hidden by tall trees.

Shortly after the accident I went on to finish my private license, then with a bush flying bug in my veins completed my commercial and headed north to seek employment.

Only once since that day did the experience come back and haunt me, and that was when I trained for a float endorsement at Whitehorse Yukon. The take off on floats was new and exciting but on final for the first touch and go when we crossed the local hydro dam power lines inbound for the water, the crash still fresh in my mind forced me to close my eyes until we were back on the lake.

For over the next 25 plus years I flew roughly 35 different aircraft types on wheels/ skis retractables and floats until the need for

Egress training in Canada became more important than being a full time pilot.

With well over 10.000 hours flying time first in the bush then to Medi-vac flights and corporate companies, until most recently 10 years of IFR single pilot Cargo, I have witnessed situations too numerous to mention all over North America and abroad.

With the enormous numbers of aircraft all over the world in flight right this moment, it is obvious that things are going to happen no matter how many safety minded and well trained pilots are.

Statistically there is an aircraft somewhere on the planet earth each and every day of the year for one reason or another that ends up ditching with pilots and passengers onboard.

In our Egress training program since 1999, I have witnessed first hand thousands of shocked faces of pilots and passengers who later agreed that the first dunking was far more complicated and challenging than expected.

Only after multiple simulated rollovers did most become comfortable in our equipment and then build confidence to egress from a cockpit inversion with out difficulty.

I highly recommend all pilots and frequent flying passengers enroll in Egress Training and experience in advance what could be a lethal situation for anyone unfamiliar with what happens during a ditching. Further to this if untrained captains are trying desperately to save themselves during an unexpected ditching, who is assisting the totally unfamiliar passengers in the back?

Thank you for taking the time to read this guide on aircraft Ditching or Egress Training and I look forward to training you.

Fly Safe

Bry The Dunker Guy

Bryan Webster

Cessna 185 North of Fort Smith, NWT
Porter Lake summer of 1996.

Bryan Webster

Founder of

AVIATION EGRESS SYSTEMS

1-250-704-6401
www.dunkyou.com
info@dunkyou.com

Training available country wide.

Amphibious Flip

This amphibious float equipped Cessna 185 as shown on cover, was only being flown a short distance near Kenora Ontario Canada September of 2004.The pilot called flight services to advise his intentions prior to landing, as the aircraft touched down with the amphibious wheels extended it abruptly overturned. The shaken but uninjured pilot was taken to hospital, examined and subsequently released.

As for the aircraft, it was removed from the lake then rebuilt and is back in the air today.

ISBN 141206902-5

9 781412 069021